betty robison

*live every day in the
freedom of Jesus Christ*

free
to be me
forty-day devotional

LIFE OUTREACH PUBLICATIONS

dedication

My prayer is that this devotional will be an inspiration and encouragement to all who read it. James, thank you for always standing by me, for being my encourager and my best friend.

I want to dedicate this book to the girls in our family: Rhonda, Robin, our daughters; Debbie, our daughter-in-law; our granddaughters, Lora, Abbie, Laney, Callie, and Audrey; and our granddaughter-in-law, Cassi, who told me specifically to drop the "in-law" part because she wanted to be considered a granddaughter. I like that!!

As a mother and grandmother, I'm so thankful for every opportunity to be an example of the freedom that only God can bring into our lives. I gladly dedicate this book to them and especially in remembrance of our daughter Robin, who has already gone to be with Jesus. She was the inspiration for the painting on the cover of this book. The painting was done by our granddaughter Abbie as a celebration of her Aunt Robin's beautiful life.

Betty Robison

ABBIE ROBISON is 21 years old and is a senior at Baylor University in Waco, Texas. She is passionate about life and loves expressing herself through her paintings.

contents

preface

In the Free to Be Me: Forty-Day Devotional,
I want to take you back through some of
my life experiences and share the moments
that impacted me forever.

As I meditated on God's Word, the Lord used
those moments to peel away years of hurt and
bring truth to the lies I had believed since
I was a child. It was in those moments that
I saw God's faithfulness, even when, in my
mind, I had been unfaithful.

I chose to write a 40-day devotional for a
very specific reason. Throughout the Bible, the

number 40 represents the transition from trial
and tribulation to rest or restoration:

~ The Israelites wandered in the desert for
40 years before entering the promised land
(Numbers 14:33-34).
~ Jesus remained on the earth for 40 days
after His resurrection before He ascended
into heaven (Acts 1:3).
~ Jesus was tempted for 40 days by
Satan (Luke 4:1-2).
~ I felt this was such a beautiful picture of
my journey. God took the years I struggled
with fear and insecurity and not only
turned them into my ministry, but He
gave me greater security, boldness, joy and
peace than I could have ever imagined. He
is altogether wonderful.

freedom is for you

The Lord gives freedom to the prisoners.

Psalm 146:7 NKJV

Have you ever felt insecure? Been afraid to fail? Felt plain and ordinary when others around you seem to be shining stars? You have to "do" in order to be someone? You don't measure up to others? You're ugly, invisible or inadequate?

If any of these secret thoughts apply to you, I want you to know that you're not alone. But it can certainly feel that way. I know, because I have struggled personally with every single one of those things.

I'm here to tell you that Jesus took me from the shackles of fear to true freedom. Although the journey took me many years, and it's not entirely over yet (because He is continually refining me), I can now boldly say that I finally have discovered the "good news:" God loves us and accepts us just as we are, right now.

Free to be the unique persons He has created us to be. And, most of all, free to pursue, without hindrance, the kind of loving relationship He longs to have with us as His children.

So today, choose to trust and believe the Lord for your freedom. Ask Him to begin to help you break free from fear and insecurity or whatever may be holding you back. He wants to give you freedom in every area of your life!

FURTHER STUDY: 2 Corinthians 3:17; John 8:36; Galatians 5:1

DECLARE TODAY:

Jesus, I receive Your freedom in my life. I receive
Your grace and mercy. Fear has no place here.
You are my security and my confidence.
Your Word is life to my body, soul and spirit.

day 2

you don't have to be good for God to love you

But God demonstrates his own love for us in this:

While we were still sinners, Christ died for us.

Romans 5:8

I have met so many people who believe they have to be "good" for God to love them. Yes, God wants our obedience, but our obedience does not determine His love for us. God loved us even before we came to Jesus. He loves us even in our sin.

For years, I lived in a prison of fear and self-doubt, paralyzed by the false thinking that God would love me only if I was good, which

12

to me translated as being busy "doing something" for Him. And yet no matter what I did, it was never enough.

After many years of struggling with self-hatred, God has graciously shown me that I don't have to be perfect to come before Him, and neither do you.

He is waiting for us, longing for intimate, two-way conversation. And He longs to show us how to break out of our individual prisons – negative thoughts, addictions, destructive patterns – He wants us free and walking in His finished work on the cross!

The more we understand all that God has done for us, the more we will live our lives to bring glory to Him.

FURTHER STUDY: Hebrews 10:10; Romans 8:37-39; 1 John 4:18

DECLARE TODAY:

Jesus, I receive Your freedom in my life. I receive Your grace and mercy. Fear has no place here.
You are my security and my confidence.
Your Word is life to my body, soul and spirit.

day 3

the power of words:
part one

Am I now trying to win the approval of men, or of God?

Or am I trying to please men? If I were still trying to

please men, I would not be a servant of Christ.

Galatians 1:10 NKJV

As a very young girl, I overheard my mother telling someone that she had asked the doctor why my head was so big and my body so small. She said when I was born, I appeared out of proportion compared to her other children. These words immediately resonated in my mind with the feelings of insignificance I already carried.

What my mother asked out of genuine concern, I allowed the enemy to use negatively in my life.

But as God revealed His thoughts of me, I learned I was created in the image of God for a purpose. I began to understand that I was unique – there was no one else like me. I realized that comparison was only a hindrance to finding my identity in the One who created me.

I encourage you to wake up every morning and thank God for the person He made you to be!

FURTHER STUDY: Psalm 139:13-16; Genesis 1:27

DECLARE TODAY:

Jesus, I receive Your freedom in my life. I receive Your grace and mercy. Fear has no place here. You are my security and my confidence. Your Word is life to my body, soul and spirit.

day 4

the power of words: part two

The tongue has the power of life and death…

Proverbs 18:21

Like me, maybe someone's words about you in the past have hurt. Or maybe you've spoken words that you wish you could take back. I learned at a very young age how much my words, and the words of others, can impact someone's life.

Just as Proverbs 18:21 says, words are powerful!

Our mouths are a gift, but it all depends how we use them. I believe God created our mouths to speak life, to encourage others and to communicate His love to everyone we encounter!

The more we use our mouths to share the love of Jesus, to lift up others and to call them to greatness, the more we will experience those things in our own lives.

FURTHER STUDY: Ephesians 4:29; Proverbs 25:11; Colossians 4:6

DECLARE TODAY:

Jesus, I receive Your freedom in my life. I receive Your grace and mercy. Fear has no place here. You are my security and my confidence. Your Word is life to my body, soul and spirit.

there is no love like the Father's love

Because your love is better than life,

my lips will glorify you.

Psalm 63:3

When I was young, the highlight of my summer was always visiting my grandparents. I received from my I'Daddy (grandfather) the attention I longed for and failed to receive from my own father at home. Wherever he was, I was never far away. I loved being around him.

I loved sitting on his lap and learning from him. I knew he loved me unconditionally.

His presence brought me so much peace and delight.

I didn't realize at that age that my relationship with I'Daddy was such a beautiful picture of the way our Heavenly Father longs for us to be close to Him. He loves to spend time with us, giving us all of His love and affection, teaching us His ways and sharing His heart.

Our Heavenly Father delights in us – think about that.

Today, rest in knowing that your Father in heaven takes delight in you.

FURTHER STUDY: Matthew 7:9-11; Isaiah 64:8; 1 John 3:1

DECLARE TODAY:

Jesus, I receive Your freedom in my life. I receive Your grace and mercy. Fear has no place here. You are my security and my confidence. Your Word is life to my body, soul and spirit.

day 6

enjoying Jesus

Come near to God and he will come near to you.

James 4:8

I have learned so much from my husband throughout our years together. Early in our relationship, even before marriage, when James was travelling frequently, he wrote me letters from the road. And in his letters, he always talked about finding a quiet place every day to spend time with God.

What was always so intriguing to me was that he never saw it as an obligation. Jesus was so real to James, and that was something I longed for. James truly loved his time with Jesus. With every letter he wrote me, I couldn't wait to hear the things God showed him during those intimate moments he had with the Lord.

Today, I know for myself the intimacy with God that James always talked about. There is no greater feeling than sitting in the presence of Jesus and allowing Him to cover me with His love, His peace and His unending goodness. To know His heart for me is beyond anything I could ever have imagined.

God longs for this kind of intimacy with every one of His children. And all we have to do is invite Him in.

FURTHER STUDY: Psalm 145:18; Jeremiah 29:13; Matthew 5:8

DECLARE TODAY:

Jesus, I receive Your freedom in my life. I receive Your grace and mercy. Fear has no place here. You are my security and my confidence. Your Word is life to my body, soul and spirit.

day 7

God's mercy is greater still

The faithful love of the Lord never ends!

His mercies never cease. Great is his faithfulness;

his mercies begin afresh each morning.

Lamentations 3:22-23 NLT

When I was in the sixth grade, my daddy gave me a tiny gold basketball he had received as a sports award when he was in high school. He put it on a chain and placed it around my neck.

I felt so honored that I had been chosen to receive it. Then one day in physical education class, I lost it. I was crushed and was convinced I had let my dad down. When I faced my father with the news, he told me I shouldn't feel bad about it. His words, while gracious, didn't help me much.

My sorrow ran too deep to accept mercy. Yet in the eyes of my father, I was already forgiven.

The same is true with our Heavenly Father. There is no mistake so great that His mercy isn't greater. If you're holding on to something from your past, don't let guilt keep you from receiving your Father's mercy.

Forgive yourself because God forgave you long ago.

FURTHER STUDY: Ephesians 2:4; Titus 3:5; Hebrews 4:16; 1 Peter 2:10

DECLARE TODAY:

Jesus, I receive Your freedom in my life. I receive Your grace and mercy. Fear has no place here. You are my security and my confidence. Your Word is life to my body, soul and spirit.

day 8

He always provides

And my God will meet all your needs according

to his glorious riches in Christ Jesus.

Philippians 4:19

The Lord never ceases to amaze me, especially
when it comes to His incredible provision. As
a young married couple over 50 years ago,
James and I did not have much money or even
a consistent income.

We spent many days wondering when
James would have another speaking opportunity so that we would have enough money to
pay rent and buy groceries. Money was tight,
but somehow we always had enough.

In those moments of wondering, the only thing we could do was trust in the faithfulness of our God. And now, looking back, those were such sweet times with the Lord. We saw His faithful hand in every area of our lives.

Whatever we need, God knows before we even ask. He always provides; sometimes it's not as quick as we would prefer, but He is always on time. All we have to do is trust and put our security in Him.

FURTHER STUDY: Matthew 6:8; Matthew 6:26; Proverbs 3:5

DECLARE TODAY:

Jesus, I receive Your freedom in my life. I receive Your grace and mercy. Fear has no place here. You are my security and my confidence. Your Word is life to my body, soul and spirit.

day 9

His ways are perfect

As for God, his way is perfect; the word of the Lord is flawless. He is a shield for all who take refuge in him.

2 Samuel 22:31

About three years after James and I had our first child, Rhonda, we began praying to have another one. When I began to experience some female related pain, James insisted that I go to the doctor. We found out I had a small tumor on my right ovary, and the doctor said I would not be able to conceive.

I began to have a strong desire to pursue adoption. We prayed about it, spoke to a lawyer and filed the necessary papers. Nine months to the day after God put adoption on my heart, a baby boy was born, and he would become our son.

I can't imagine our lives without Randy. He is such a gift to our family, and I'm so thankful God orchestrated his adoption. God truly knew that this little boy would bless our family, and I wouldn't have had it any other way.

God took our disappointment and turned it into unexplainable joy! Whenever you face disappointment, know that God wants to do the same for you and turn it into joy!

FURTHER STUDY: 2 Corinthians 5:7; Isaiah 55:9; Psalm 30:11

DECLARE TODAY:

Jesus, I receive Your freedom in my life. I receive Your grace and mercy. Fear has no place here. You are my security and my confidence. Your Word is life to my body, soul and spirit.

....

....

....

....

....

....

....

....

....

....

....

....

....

....

....

....

day 10

no greater love

…so that Christ may dwell in your hearts through faith. And I pray that you, being rooted and established in love, may have power, together with all the saints, to grasp how wide and long and high and deep is the love of Christ…

Ephesians 3:17-18

As a young mother, I cherished those quiet moments with my children as I held them in my arms. When I had Rhonda, our very first child, I couldn't imagine loving another baby as much as I loved her. But when we adopted Randy, it was as if my love somehow expanded.

My entire life I had believed that God somehow had favorites. But as I held our second child in my arms, I began to understand for the first time just a glimpse of the way God loves us.

His love is vast. He has no favorites. Just as I imagined that my children could never comprehend the greatness of my love for them, we could never fathom the depth of God's love for us. His love has no limits.

Meditate on God's love for you today. God has enough love to make every single one of us feel as though we are His only child. His love is like no other.

FURTHER STUDY: 1 John 3:1; Isaiah 49:15; Ephesians 2:4-5

DECLARE TODAY:

Jesus, I receive Your freedom in my life. I receive Your grace and mercy. Fear has no place here. You are my security and my confidence. Your Word is life to my body, soul and spirit.

....

....

....

....

....

....

....

....

....

....

....

....

....

....

....

....

....

....

....

day 11

beyond all we could ask or imagine

Delight yourself in the Lord and he will

give you the desires of your heart.

Psalm 37:4

Our third child, Robin, was a miracle!

After being told that I would not be able to give birth to any more children, James and I were shocked when we found out we were pregnant again. When we adopted Randy, I had accepted the fact that another pregnancy was not an option, and I was perfectly content with two beautiful children.

But God had not forgotten the desire I once carried in my heart. He simply had a greater plan. We could see His wisdom in bringing each of our children in His timing and order.

What we often believe to be the best pales in comparison to God's best. He always goes above and beyond all we could ask or imagine.

If you're facing disappointment or heartache, know that God has not forgotten the desires of your heart. Continue to seek Him and trust the dreams He has put in your heart. His best is worth waiting for!

FURTHER STUDY: Isaiah 55:9; Ephesians 3:20; Zechariah 9:12

DECLARE TODAY:

*Jesus, I receive Your freedom in my life. I receive
Your grace and mercy. Fear has no place here.
You are my security and my confidence.
Your Word is life to my body, soul and spirit.*

day 12

Jesus has qualified you

For we are God's workmanship, created in
Christ Jesus to do good works, which God
prepared in advance for us to do.

Ephesians 2:10

Before I really experienced God's freedom and
love in my life, I often asked God why He
chose me to be James' wife. In my mind, I was
so plain and ordinary. There was nothing spe-
cial about me. I wondered what I had to offer
a man like James who was so gifted by God.
But in God's eyes, I was perfect for James.

Today, maybe you feel unqualified for the
thing God is calling you to.

God's Word says He will not call us to anything He has not already equipped us to do or be.

Through Jesus Christ, you are qualified. It is not our perfection that matters but His.

FURTHER STUDY: 2 Timothy 3:16-17; Hebrews 13:20-21; Philippians 1:6

DECLARE TODAY:

Jesus, I receive Your freedom in my life. I receive Your grace and mercy. Fear has no place here. You are my security and my confidence. Your Word is life to my body, soul and spirit.

day 13

God is never far away

For I am convinced that neither death nor life, neither

angels nor demons, neither the present nor the future,

nor any powers, neither height nor depth, nor anything

else in all creation, will be able to separate us from the

love of God that is in Christ Jesus our Lord.

Romans 8:38-39

It was years ago, but I will never forget the time that James told me he felt separated from God. I can still remember it like it was yesterday. I didn't understand how someone who was always so close to the Lord now felt so distant and disconnected.

Have you ever felt that way?

The enemy wants us to believe that we are distant from God. Satan's single greatest desire is to separate us from our source of abundant life.

But God's Word says that there is nothing that can separate us from His love. God does not move, and He is the same yesterday, today and forever.

FURTHER STUDY: Hebrews 13:8; James 1:17; James 4:8

DECLARE TODAY:

Jesus, I receive Your freedom in my life. I receive Your grace and mercy. Fear has no place here. You are my security and my confidence. Your Word is life to my body, soul and spirit.

day 14

you can hear God

My sheep hear My voice, and
I know them, and they follow Me.

John 10:27 NKJV

For many years, I believed I couldn't hear God the same way James did. Yet, I never seemed to have any trouble hearing what the enemy had to say to me. It was always negative, condemning and discouraging.

I didn't know how to hear God or understand how He speaks. I was *doing* everything I knew to do to try to hear from God. What I didn't realize is that hearing from God is not about a method or doing all the right things.

I could hear from God just like James. I just had to believe that God wanted to speak to me.

The same is true for you. Don't let the enemy convince you God doesn't speak to you; He does.

It only takes us quieting ourselves before Him and asking Him to speak to us through His Word and by His Spirit.

FURTHER STUDY: 2 Timothy 3:16-17; Job 33:14; Romans 10:17

DECLARE TODAY:

Jesus, I receive Your freedom in my life. I receive Your grace and mercy. Fear has no place here. You are my security and my confidence. Your Word is life to my body, soul and spirit.

p.s. maybe God wants to speak to you

…for it will not be you speaking, but the Spirit of your Father speaking through you.

Matthew 10:20

When our youngest child, Robin, was around the age of 10, she made a card for me that read, "Dear Mom, I am praying that you will get well soon. P.S. Maybe God is trying to tell you something."

I had been living with a headache for days, so I asked James if he really thought God was trying to show me something.

James proceeded to tell me that he believed God was trying to show me that I was unteachable. While I didn't like what James was telling me, I realized it really might be true. While I don't believe God makes us sick to teach us things, I do believe God brings good out of the bad in our lives.

I got on my knees and began to weep. I confessed my unteachable spirit to the Lord. Within seconds, I opened my eyes, and my headache was gone.

God speaks to all of us in different ways…mostly through His Word and by His Spirit, but sometimes He speaks to us even through our children.

FURTHER STUDY: Job 33:14; Numbers 22:28-30; Psalm 8:2

DECLARE TODAY:

Jesus, I receive Your freedom in my life. I receive Your grace and mercy. Fear has no place here. You are my security and my confidence. Your Word is life to my body, soul and spirit.

day 16

His Word is freedom

I sought the Lord, and he answered me;

he delivered me from all my fears.

Psalm 34:4

For most of my life, fear and insecurity con-
trolled everything I said and did. Anyone
could see the hold it had on me.

When I began to expose my fear and insecurity to the Word of God, I finally realized
that I had been the target of the devil's lies
for years.

For the first time, I could actually feel God
loving on me. The barrier was gone. The more

I read His Word and had faith in what I was reading, the more freedom I experienced.

God's Word demolishes every stronghold.

If there is something holding you back, an obstacle you can't seem to get past, immerse yourself in God's Word. His Word is all the freedom and power you need to overcome your struggle. God will bring your victory.

FURTHER STUDY: 2 Corinthians 10:4-5; 2 Timothy 3:16; Hebrews 4:12

DECLARE TODAY:

Jesus, I receive Your freedom in my life. I receive Your grace and mercy. Fear has no place here. You are my security and my confidence. Your Word is life to my body, soul and spirit.

....

....

....

....

....

....

....

....

....

....

....

....

....

....

....

....

day 17

our weakness,
His strength

But he said to me, "My grace is sufficient for you, for my power is made perfect in weakness." Therefore I will boast all the more gladly about my weakness, so that Christ's power may rest on me.

2 Corinthians 12:9

It's a question I've asked myself countless times. Why would God call someone like me to be in the limelight? I didn't like being the center of attention one bit. I was perfectly fine with being in the background.

To this very day, I'm not fond of being in the limelight, but I have realized it's in those times, when I have to step out of my comfort zone, that I see God do the most.

God wants to display His power in and through our weakness. Only in Him can we do all that He has called us to. Confess your weakness, give it to Jesus and watch Him step in and do something great!

FURTHER STUDY: 1 Chronicles 16:11; Psalm 61:1-4; Psalm 147:5

DECLARE TODAY:

Jesus, I receive Your freedom in my life. I receive Your grace and mercy. Fear has no place here. You are my security and my confidence. Your Word is life to my body, soul and spirit.

free to worship

Praise his name with dancing,

accompanied by tambourine and harp.

Psalm 149:3 NLT

As a little girl, when no one was home to watch, I dressed up in a pink ballerina costume with matching ballet slippers. Lost in my own little world, I danced and twirled in our backyard, trying so hard to imitate dance movements I had seen other girls do. I sang songs to Jesus and freely expressed my love to Him without a care in the world.

I never felt so free to worship Him as I did in those moments. It was just me and Jesus.

To this day, I go to Jesus like a child longing for the Father's embrace. The Bible says that God inhabits the praises of His people.

God longs for every single one of us to worship Him in this way – to abandon our surroundings and the pressures of life and just enjoy singing and dancing in His presence.

Don't worry about who might walk in or what they might think. Just focus on Jesus and dance!

FURTHER STUDY: Psalm 100:1-5; Psalm 150:1-6; Psalm 146:1-2

DECLARE TODAY:

Jesus, I receive Your freedom in my life. I receive Your grace and mercy. Fear has no place here. You are my security and my confidence. Your Word is life to my body, soul and spirit.

day 19

God wants to use me?

*…who comforts us in all our troubles, so that
we can comfort those in any trouble with the
comfort we ourselves receive from God.*

2 Corinthians 1:4

When the Lord truly delivered me from my
fear and insecurity, James began sharing at
our Bible Conferences what God had done
in my life.

It wasn't long before I received my first
invitation to speak to a group of women.
In the past, I would have turned down the
opportunity right away, but suddenly, I had a
strong desire to share what God had done in

my life. I was excited to tell others they could experience the freedom I had found.

During that time, I learned God wants to help us overcome our struggles so He can use us to help others find His freedom and comfort, too. God likes to take our mess and make it our ministry.

God wants you to be more than a conqueror. And He wants you to be a carrier of His power and love in all you do.

FURTHER STUDY: 2 Corinthians 12:9; Ephesians 2:10; James 1:2-4

DECLARE TODAY:

Jesus, I receive Your freedom in my life. I receive Your grace and mercy. Fear has no place here. You are my security and my confidence. Your Word is life to my body, soul and spirit.

day 20

one verse at a time

May the God of hope fill you with all joy and peace

as you trust in him, so that you may overflow with

hope by the power of the Holy Spirit.

Romans 15:13

My new-found freedom in Christ brought
about an excitement for God's Word that I had
never experienced.

It was amazing…suddenly my heart was
filled with hope and expectation of great things!
I couldn't get enough. I craved His Word.

As I took one verse at a time and meditated
on it, asking God to show me His truth, He

gave me understanding. With every verse that He unfolded, I wanted more.

God wants to do the same for you. You don't have to start off reading an entire book of the Bible. Pick one verse and focus on it for the day. Ask the Lord to speak to you through it. He will.

There is so much life to be discovered in His Word!

FURTHER STUDY: Psalm 119:105; John 17:17; John 1:1-2

DECLARE TODAY:

Jesus, I receive Your freedom in my life. I receive Your grace and mercy. Fear has no place here. You are my security and my confidence. Your Word is life to my body, soul and spirit.

His Word is alive

"Every word of God is flawless; he is a shield
to those who take refuge in him."

Proverbs 30:5

The more I immersed myself in God's Word, the more I became obsessed with seeing His truth and hearing Him on my own, something I never thought possible.

Studying God's Word changed my thoughts, my faith and my enjoyment of life. For every question I had, God's Word held the answer.

God desires for His Word to abide in everyone's heart, and when it does, we find ourselves thinking differently, thinking positively and loving others with the love that He has shown us. It isn't something we conjure up on our own, but it is His power at work in our lives.

His Word really is alive, and the fruit is effortless on our part!

FURTHER STUDY: Hebrews 4:12; Isaiah 55:11; 2 Timothy 3:16

DECLARE TODAY:

Jesus, I receive Your freedom in my life. I receive Your grace and mercy. Fear has no place here.
You are my security and my confidence.
Your Word is life to my body, soul and spirit.

day 22

God loves you as much as...

*"I do not pray for these alone, but also for those who will believe in Me through their word; that they all may be one, as You, Father, are in Me, and I in You; that they also may be one in Us, that the world may believe that You sent Me. And the glory which You gave Me I have given them, that they may be one just as We are one: I in them, and You in Me; that they may be made perfect in one, and that the world may know that You have sent Me, and **have loved them as You have loved Me.**"*

John 17:20-23 NKJV

When God brought freedom to my life, I began to see evidence of His great love for me throughout the Bible in everything I read. It is astounding to me that God's own Son prayed that we would know our Father's love as He knew it.

Only when we begin to understand just how much God loved His Son can we begin to grasp how much God loves us.

FURTHER STUDY: John 3:16; John 3:1-3; Romans 5:8

DECLARE TODAY:

Jesus, I receive Your freedom in my life. I receive Your grace and mercy. Fear has no place here. You are my security and my confidence. Your Word is life to my body, soul and spirit.

we have already won!

I have hidden your word in my heart
that I might not sin against you.

Psalm 119:11

When James and I made the decision to home-school our youngest daughter, Robin, for her senior year of high school, many of the insecurities I thought I had overcome returned.

The enemy played the same tape again in my head – "You are dumb. You never excelled academically. Robin is only a teenager, and she is more intelligent than you are." The voice was all too familiar.

But this time around, I knew they were lies. The truth of God's Word had taken root in my heart.

I knew that my battle was already won. My job was to claim my victory! God's Word is our weapon. When we face trials, His truth emerges within our hearts.

Remember, our battle is not against flesh and blood but against princes and principalities of darkness.

FURTHER STUDY: Ephesians 6:12-17; Exodus 14:14; 2 Corinthians 10:3-5

DECLARE TODAY:

Jesus, I receive Your freedom in my life. I receive Your grace and mercy. Fear has no place here. You are my security and my confidence. Your Word is life to my body, soul and spirit.

day 24

rest for the weary

*Take my yoke upon you and learn from
me, for I am gentle and humble in heart,
and you will find rest for your souls.*

Matthew 11:29

Carrying the weight of insecurity and fear is
exhausting. I would know…I carried it for
over 20 years. I never felt good enough.
I always was striving to be better, to do
more and to measure up.

But when God set me free, it was like a
breath of fresh air. God quieted my mind
through His Word and set my worries at ease.

God wanted me – body, soul and spirit – to be at rest.

Only when we are at rest within our spirit are we free to be all that God has called us to be.

FURTHER STUDY: Jeremiah 31:25; Isaiah 26:3; 2 Corinthians 10:3-5

DECLARE TODAY:

Jesus, I receive Your freedom in my life. I receive Your grace and mercy. Fear has no place here. You are my security and my confidence. Your Word is life to my body, soul and spirit.

God's not done with me yet

"For I know the plans I have for you," declares the Lord, "plans to prosper you and not to harm you, plans to give you hope and a future."

Jeremiah 29:11

When the wonderful season of mothering and caring for my three children at home was coming to an end and I realized James and I soon would be empty-nesters, my heart wanted to feel lost.

I thought to myself, "What purpose do I have now?"

In that moment of loneliness, I knew the Lord wanted to speak to me. His nearness was so clear. He impressed on my heart that He still had plans for me. I felt that He was calling me into a new season of ministry with James. And the months following proved that to be true.

Through every season of our lives, the good and the bad, God is faithful. He never leaves us. He never forsakes us. And His plans for us always surpass our greatest expectations.

FURTHER STUDY: Ecclesiastes 3:1-22; Isaiah 58:11; Psalm 37:23

DECLARE TODAY:

Jesus, I receive Your freedom in my life. I receive Your grace and mercy. Fear has no place here. You are my security and my confidence. Your Word is life to my body, soul and spirit.

day 26

my very best friend

We love because he first loved us.

1 John 4:19

James and I have always loved spending time together. We really are best friends. Our relationship has always been a priority. We take time to nurture it and do our best to communicate our love to one another.

James' love for me has been such a beautiful representation of God's love for me.

He pursues my heart…just like Jesus does.

But as much as I know my husband loves me, nothing compares to the love that Jesus has lavished on me.

Every moment of every day, Jesus is chasing us. He gave up His life for us. He wants to talk to us. He wants to love on us. He wants to lead us. He wants to be our very best friend.

FURTHER STUDY: John 15:13-16; Psalm 23:6; 1 Corinthians 13:4-8

DECLARE TODAY:

Jesus, I receive Your freedom in my life. I receive Your grace and mercy. Fear has no place here. You are my security and my confidence. Your Word is life to my body, soul and spirit.

day 27

I am with you

"This is my command – be strong and courageous!
Do not be afraid or discouraged. For the Lord your
God is with you wherever you go."

Joshua 1:9 NLT

When God put missions on James' heart and
LIFE Outreach began raising funds for missions
in Africa, James and I traveled there frequently.

Travelling always made me nervous, and at
times, certain areas of South Africa were very
unstable and dangerous. But I loved interact-
ing with the precious African people, and I
was so thankful we were able to do something
to help them.

I remember praying that God would not "call" us to live there, and hearing Him reply, "Betty, if I called you to live there, you would have peace, and I would equip you with everything you need."

The Lord never called us to live in Africa, but I learned a very valuable lesson.

God will never send us somewhere without His peace, provision and protection. Even if He takes us somewhere that is a little scary, we will always have peace in knowing He is with us every step of the way.

FURTHER STUDY: Hebrews 13:21; Isaiah 30:21; Isaiah 41:10

DECLARE TODAY:

Jesus, I receive Your freedom in my life. I receive Your grace and mercy. Fear has no place here. You are my security and my confidence. Your Word is life to my body, soul and spirit.

day 28

the joy of knowing Jesus

A cheerful heart is good medicine,

but a crushed spirit dries up the bones.

Proverbs 17:22

Great joy is found when we express our praise and gratitude to the Lord. Even in the midst of the worst possible circumstances, praise has the power to change everything.

I saw this firsthand in the country of Sudan, Africa, years ago. When our team landed and got off the plane in Sudan, we were greeted by some of the happiest people I've ever met. They were singing praises to Jesus for our safe arrival.

These people were living in some of the worst conditions I'd ever seen...extreme poverty, suffocating heat and very little water. It was heartbreaking. And not only were the living conditions bad, Christians all over the country were being massacred by Muslim extremists.

In that moment, I was reminded that Jesus truly is life and joy. We may not have clothes, food, water or shelter, but a heart of gratitude brings joy in the midst of dire circumstances. And praising the name of Jesus brings life to our bodies and our spirits and releases God's power into our lives.

He is ALL we need.

FURTHER STUDY: Psalm 4:7; Acts 16:16-35; Psalm 21:6

DECLARE TODAY:

Jesus, I receive Your freedom in my life. I receive
Your grace and mercy. Fear has no place here.
You are my security and my confidence.
Your Word is life to my body, soul and spirit.

....

....

....

....

....

....

....

....

....

....

....

day 29

worry or rest?

But those who wait on the Lord shall renew

their strength; They shall mount up with wings

like eagles, They shall run and not be weary,

They shall walk and not faint.

Isaiah 40:31 NKJV

The world around us tells us we need to be strong, to be more disciplined and not to let the troubles of life get us down. But, most of the time, life does get to us, and we are left feeling like failures when our own strength, effort and self-control isn't enough.

Life gives us plenty of opportunities to worry... when we have a sick child, when a loved one is diagnosed with a fatal illness or simply when life just doesn't go the way we think it should.

In those moments, we have a choice to make. We can choose to rely on our own strength, which would leave us feeling tired, worried and useless. Or we can choose to rely on God's strength and rest in Him.

My prayer is that in every situation, we would choose to find our strength in Him and trust that He is going to bring peace to our circumstances and rest to our hearts.

FURTHER STUDY: Matthew 11:28-30; 2 Corinthians 12:9-10; Ephesians 6:10

DECLARE TODAY:

Jesus, I receive Your freedom in my life. I receive Your grace and mercy. Fear has no place here. You are my security and my confidence. Your Word is life to my body, soul and spirit.

day 30

the God of miracles

And we know that in all things God works
for the good of those who love him, who have
been called according to his purpose.

Romans 8:28

One particular mission trip, James and I went
to the country of Angola, Africa. Everything
on the trip went smoothly until the last day.
We were headed to a refugee camp when all of
the sudden, a group of military men swarmed
our van. We were held at gunpoint for several
minutes.

Albert, the local missionary with us, convinced the soldiers to take him to speak with

the Colonel. Albert returned with the Colonel, who then personally escorted us back to the camp to finish passing out supplies to the refugees.

We went from being prisoners held at gunpoint to having a military escort to finish the job God called us to. We were amazed!

There are many things that happen in our lives we don't understand, but no moment is wasted when it is given to God for His glorious outcome. He can turn around any situation!

FURTHER STUDY: John 16:33;
1 Corinthians 10:13; Psalm 9:10

DECLARE TODAY:

Jesus, I receive Your freedom in my life. I receive Your grace and mercy. Fear has no place here. You are my security and my confidence. Your Word is life to my body, soul and spirit.

it's time to enjoy your life

There is no fear in love. But perfect love drives
out fear, because fear has to do with punishment.
The one who fears is not made perfect in love.

1 John 4:18

I never understood why my earthly father
didn't show affection toward his children.
I knew he loved me, but he struggled to
express it physically.

Years down the road, I found out that he,
too, battled insecurity. To this day, I wonder
how different my relationship with my dad
could have been if somehow he could have

known the God I know now – the God who frees us to love Him and love life.

Insecurity keeps us from truly experiencing our lives and enjoying the people we love.

If you struggle with insecurity, it's time for you to enjoy your life.

Place your worth and security in Jesus. Renew your mind with who His Word says you are. It's not about what you do; it's about who *HE* is.

FURTHER STUDY: John 8:36; Matthew 6:25-34; Deuteronomy 33:12

DECLARE TODAY:

Jesus, I receive Your freedom in my life. I receive Your grace and mercy. Fear has no place here. You are my security and my confidence. Your Word is life to my body, soul and spirit.

....

....

....

....

....

....

....

....

....

....

....

day 32

He stays the same

So do not fear, for I am with you; do not be dismayed,

for I am your God. I will strengthen you and help

you; I will uphold you with my righteous right hand.

Isaiah 41:10

We were designed for relationship...with God
and with one another.

I learned a great deal about my relationship
with God during the last year of my mother's
life as she struggled with Alzheimer's disease.
We had always been so close, but it was as if
I didn't even know her anymore. She was no
longer the strong-willed, confident woman she
once was.

I didn't know how to respond to her emotions and condition changing daily.

However, my changing relationship with my mother increased my confidence in God. He alone became my strength and my source. I desperately needed His guidance and His wisdom.

I can say this about so many relationships I've had throughout my life, good or bad. I always come to a greater realization of God's unchanging love for me.

No earthly relationship could ever replace our relationship with God. When the people and circumstances around us change, He stays the same.

FURTHER STUDY: Numbers 23:19; 1 Chronicles 16:11; Psalm 73:26

DECLARE TODAY:

Jesus, I receive Your freedom in my life. I receive Your grace and mercy. Fear has no place here. You are my security and my confidence. Your Word is life to my body, soul and spirit.

....

....

....

....

....

....

....

....

....

....

....

....

....

....

....

....

....

day 33

don't forget
to look around

A word fitly spoken is like apples

of gold in settings of silver.

Proverbs 25:11 NKJV

We live in a world that never stops to breathe. We are so busy doing this and doing that, we forget to look around. We forget to ask ourselves, "Who around us might need some encouragement?"

Freedom in Christ causes us to look beyond ourselves.

I don't ever want to get so busy that I pass up an individual who needs to hear me say,

"God put some good things in you. He cares about you with all of His heart, and He wants to lead and direct your steps."

Let's not allow fear keep us from letting the light of Jesus Christ shine through. I want to challenge you to be willing to bring the "God-colors" into someone else's life. We have the opportunity to be a part of changing lives for eternity.

Don't forget to look around!

FURTHER STUDY: 1 Thessalonians 5:11; Acts 20:35; Philemon 1:6

DECLARE TODAY:

Jesus, I receive Your freedom in my life. I receive Your grace and mercy. Fear has no place here. You are my security and my confidence. Your Word is life to my body, soul and spirit.

....

....

....

....

....

....

....

....

....

....

day 34

there is no fear in love

Ears that hear and eyes that see
– the Lord has made them both.

Proverbs 20:12

As I read in Proverbs 20:12 how having ears to hear and eyes to see is a gift from God, I asked Him to help me hear, see and be more mindful of people around me.

Shortly after this, I was walking into the pharmacy and saw a lady sitting outside who looked so sad. I recognized her as a pharmacy employee I had seen before. Normally, I would have avoided eye contact and walked straight in, but I knew the Lord was prompting me

140

to pray with her and express His love to her. I simply asked her what was wrong, and she began to weep. We prayed together, and I believe the Lord really touched her that day.

Sometimes people just need to know someone cares. I was so thankful God wanted to use me.

I recall so many times I passed up an opportunity to pray with someone or speak encouragement when I saw a need.

Let's forget about the inconvenience and fear of failure or embarrassment when it comes to loving others. When you see a person in need, remember that love breaks all barriers, and God will give you the boldness you need to touch someone with His love.

FURTHER STUDY: 2 Corinthians 3:7-18; Hebrews 13:6; 1 John 4:18

DECLARE TODAY:

Jesus, I receive Your freedom in my life. I receive Your grace and mercy. Fear has no place here. You are my security and my confidence. Your Word is life to my body, soul and spirit.

day 35

we win; fear loses

*For God has not given us a spirit of fear, but
of power and of love and of a sound mind.*

2 Timothy 1:7 NKJV

Years ago, our television staff planned a show
where the employees of our ministry filled
the audience. They were allowed to ask James
and me any question on any topic – spiritual,
marital, ethical or even personal.

I was so nervous. What if they asked me
something I did not know the answer to? In
the past, because of fear, I would never have
agreed to do something like this, but this time,
I was determined to go through with it.

I prayed for God's wisdom and insight to guide my responses.

To my surprise, the show went great. I responded to all the questions that came my way with ease, and once again, God had proven Himself faithful to me. In my weakness, He was strong. Fear no longer had control.

If you need courage today, meditate on 2 Timothy 1:7. God has not given you a spirit of fear. You can overcome and walk in confidence that God is who He says He is, and God does what He says He will do.

FURTHER STUDY: John 14:27; Mark 5:36; Psalm 34:4

DECLARE TODAY:

Jesus, I receive Your freedom in my life. I receive Your grace and mercy. Fear has no place here. You are my security and my confidence. Your Word is life to my body, soul and spirit.

stepping out in God's confidence

Not that we are competent in ourselves

to claim anything for ourselves,

but our competence comes from God.

2 Corinthians 3:5

Very early in my life, I built up walls to keep anyone from truly knowing me. I was afraid that if they really knew me, they would discover my insecurity.

I figured the more discipline and self-control I displayed, the more secure and safe my life would be.

But when God broke through my fear, I realized that pride was holding me captive in my fear. It wasn't until I admitted I had needs and couldn't do it on my own that the walls came down.

But my breakthrough didn't happen overnight.

You can stop striving. Stop performing. Breakthroughs come when we choose to hold tightly to God's hand and step out in *His* confidence, not our own.

FURTHER STUDY: Proverbs 11:2; James 4:6; Proverbs 3:26

DECLARE TODAY:

Jesus, I receive Your freedom in my life. I receive Your grace and mercy. Fear has no place here. You are my security and my confidence. Your Word is life to my body, soul and spirit.

day 37

as Jesus was, we are:
part one

Read the verses below and ask the Lord to speak to you through them.

Don't worry about anything; instead, pray about

everything. Tell God what you need, and thank

him for all he has done. Then you will experience

God's peace, which exceeds anything we can

understand. His peace will guard your hearts and

minds as you live in Christ Jesus.

And now, dear brothers and sisters, one final

thing. Fix your thoughts on what is true, and

honorable, and right, and pure, and lovely, and

admirable. Think about things that are excellent

and worthy of praise. Keep putting into practice

all you learned and received from me – everything

you heard from me and saw me doing.

Then the God of peace will be with you.

Philippians 4:6-9 NLT

Jesus came and gave His life so we can have His mind and know His thoughts in order to live as He did on this earth – FREE.

FURTHER STUDY: Romans 8:2-8; 2 Peter 1:4-9; Romans 6:1-14

DECLARE TODAY:

Jesus, I receive Your freedom in my life. I receive Your grace and mercy. Fear has no place here. You are my security and my confidence. Your Word is life to my body, soul and spirit.

day 38

as Jesus was, we are: part two

*The thief comes only to steal and kill
and destroy; I have come that they
may have life, and have it to the full.*

John 10:10

God is calling us to step into a new realm of living where we allow Jesus to give us the abundant life He has promised in His Word. If we open our minds and hearts, **His** words will have an amazing effect on our inner selves.

His words will affect our attitude, confidence, joy, health and relationships. And, through Jesus' sacrificial death on the cross, the power of these life-changing words is available to anyone who chooses to seek a personal relationship with Him.

Jesus is our supply to all of life's demands. There is nothing He cannot do, no need He cannot meet and no burden He cannot lift!

The Bible references below are the same as the previous devotional, but I encourage you to read them again and give the Lord opportunity to speak.

FURTHER STUDY: Romans 8:2-8; 2 Peter 1:4-9; Romans 6:1-14

DECLARE TODAY:

Jesus, I receive Your freedom in my life. I receive Your grace and mercy. Fear has no place here. You are my security and my confidence. Your Word is life to my body, soul and spirit.

salvation by grace

For it is by grace you have been saved, through faith –
and this not from yourselves, it is the gift of God.

Ephesians 2:8

One of the greatest aspects of our faith in Jesus Christ we can come to understand is the importance of salvation by grace.

Growing up, I did all the religious things that I thought I needed to do. I was faithful in church attendance, and by the book of the law, I lived a very religious life.

I thought that if I didn't, then God wouldn't love me.

You need to know that salvation is a free gift. It can't be earned by our good works – by doing noble or religious acts for God and others. There is no way we can earn God's love and acceptance.

Open your heart to God's gift of grace – it's free!

FURTHER STUDY: Ephesians 1:7; Romans 3:24; Ephesians 2:8-9

DECLARE TODAY:

Jesus, I receive Your freedom in my life. I receive Your grace and mercy. Fear has no place here. You are my security and my confidence. Your Word is life to my body, soul and spirit.

day 40

our only source
of true security

"Then you will know the truth,

and the truth will set you free."

John 8:32

Security...all of us are looking for it one way or another. We look for it in our relationships, our jobs, our social status and especially our finances.

In the very beginning of my marrriage with James, I looked to James for affirmation in everything I did. Then came the dark years in which my confident husband struggled through layers of defeat and looked to me for strength and hope.

But I had nothing to offer. For so long, I had depended on James instead of the Lord.

I know now that God used that period in our lives to cause me to turn my focus toward Him. God was our only hope. When I ran to Him, I discovered that in His loving arms was the place I should have been all along.

God was, is and always will be the only source of real and lasting security.

FURTHER STUDY: Psalm 40:2; Psalm 39:7; Proverbs 3:26

DECLARE TODAY:

Jesus, I receive Your freedom in my life. I receive Your grace and mercy. Fear has no place here. You are my security and my confidence. Your Word is life to my body, soul and spirit.

Free to Be Me: Forty-Day Devotional

Copyright © 2014 by Inprov, Ltd.

ISBN: 978-0-9914820-9-2

For further information, write to
Inprov
2150 E. Continental Blvd.
Southlake, TX 76092

Unless otherwise noted, all scripture references taken from THE HOLY BIBLE, NEW INTERNATIONAL VERSION®, NIV®, Copyright © 1973, 1978, 1984, 2011 by Biblica, Inc.™ Used by permission. All rights reserved worldwide.

Scripture quotations marked NKJV are taken from the New King James Version®, Copyright © 1982 by Thomas Nelson, Inc. Used by permission. All rights reserved.

Scripture quotations marked NLT are taken from the Holy Bible, New Living Translation, Copyright © 1996, 2004, 2007 by Tyndale House Foundation. Used by permission of Tyndale House Publishers, Inc., Carol Stream, Illinois 60188. All rights reserved.